Collins English Readers

Amazing Mathematicians

Level 2
CEF A2–B1

Text by
Anna Trewin

Collins

HarperCollins Publishers
77–85 Fulham Palace Road
Hammersmith London W6 8JB

10 9 8 7 6 5 4 3 2 1

Original text
© The Amazing People Club Ltd

Adapted text
© HarperCollins Publishers Ltd 2014

ISBN: 978-0-00-754503-2

Collins® is a registered trademark of
HarperCollins Publishers Limited

www.collinselt.com

A catalogue record for this book is available
from the British Library

Printed in the UK by Martins the Printers

These readers are based on original texts
(BioViews®) published by The Amazing
People Club group.® BioViews® and The
Amazing People Club® are registered
trademarks and represent the views of the
author.

BioViews® are scripted virtual interview
based on research about a person's life and
times. As in any story, the words are only
an interpretation of what the individuals
mentioned in the BioViews® could have
said. Although the interpretations are
based on available research, they do not
purport to represent the actual views of
the people mentioned. The interpretations
are made in good faith, recognizing
that other interpretations could also be
made. The author and publisher disclaim
any responsibility from any action that
readers take regarding the BioViews® for
educational or other purposes. Any use
of the BioViews® materials is the sole
responsibility of the reader and should
be supported by their own independent
research.

Cover image © Ugorenkov Aleksandr/
Shutterstock

MIX
Paper from
responsible sources
FSC **FSC™ C007454**
www.fsc.org

FSC™ is a non-profit international organisation established to promote the
responsible management of the world's forests. Products carrying the FSC
label are independently certified to assure consumers that they come from
forests that are managed to meet the social, economic and ecological needs
of present and future generations, and other controlled sources.

Find out more about HarperCollins and the environment at
www.harpercollins.co.uk/green

✦ Contents ✦

◆ Introduction ◆

Collins Amazing People Readers are collections of short stories. Each book presents the life story of five or six people whose lives and achievements have made a difference to our world today. The stories are carefully graded to ensure that you, the reader, will both enjoy and benefit from your reading experience.

You can choose to enjoy the book from start to finish or to dip into your favourite story straight away. Each story is entirely independent.

After every story a short timeline brings together the most important events in each person's life into one short report. The timeline is a useful tool for revision purposes.

Words which are above the required reading level are underlined the first time they appear in each story. All underlined words are defined in the glossary at the back of the book. Levels 1 and 2 take their definitions from the *Collins COBUILD Essential English Dictionary* and levels 3 and 4 from the *Collins COBUILD Advanced English Dictionary*.

To support both teachers and learners, additional materials are available online at www.collinselt.com/readers.

The Amazing People Club®

Collins Amazing People Readers are adaptations of original texts published by The Amazing People Club. The Amazing People Club is an educational publishing house. It was founded in 2006 by educational psychologist and management leader Dr Charles Margerison and publishes books, eBooks, audio books, iBooks and video content, which bring readers 'face to face' with many of the world's most inspiring and influential characters from the fields of art, science, music, politics, medicine and business.

◆ THE GRADING SCHEME ◆

The Collins COBUILD Grading Scheme has been created using the most up-to-date language usage information available today. Each level is guided by a brand new comprehensive grammar and vocabulary framework, ensuring that the series will perfectly match readers' abilities.

		CEF band	Pages	Word count	Headwords
Level 1	elementary	A2	64	5,000–8,000	approx. 700
Level 2	pre-intermediate	A2–B1	80	8,000–11,000	approx. 900
Level 3	intermediate	B1	96	11,000–15,000	approx. 1,100
Level 4	upper intermediate	B2	112	15,000–19,000	approx. 1,700

For more information on the Collins COBUILD Grading Scheme, including a full list of the grammar structures found at each level, go to www.collinselt.com/readers/gradingscheme.

Also available online: Make sure that you are reading at the right level by checking your level on our website (www.collinselt.com/readers/levelcheck).

Galileo

◆ ◆ ◆

1564–1642

the man who believed the Earth
went around the Sun

I believed that the Earth <u>orbited</u> the Sun. People were afraid of my <u>theories</u> at the time and called me a <u>heretic</u>. But now they call me 'The Father of Modern Science'.

◆ ◆ ◆

I was born in Pisa, Italy, in 1564. I was the oldest of six children, but unfortunately, only three of us <u>survived</u> childhood. My father, Vincenzo Galilei, was a well-known musician and he called me Galileo. When I was 8 years old, my family moved to Florence. But they left me behind in Pisa, in the care of a relative. In 1574, I joined my family. When I was 11 years old, I was sent to the Camaldoese Monastery school in the town of Vallombrosa, just outside Florence.

My father wanted me to be a doctor. So, after I finished school, I went on to study medicine at the University of Pisa. However, I soon decided that medicine was not the right career for me. I was much more interested in mathematics, physics and the <u>arts</u>. So I spoke to my father and he let me change my course to mathematics and natural <u>philosophy</u>.

One day, while I was at the university, I noticed something interesting. I was looking up at the ceiling and watching a lamp swinging – or moving from side to side. The length of the lamp's swing from side to side changed with the wind coming through the open window. I noticed that the lamp always took the same number of seconds to complete its swing from one side to the other.

When I returned home, I set up two <u>pendulums</u> and <u>carried out</u> some experiments. Soon I realized that I had discovered a truth – that all things swing at the same speed. This was later called 'the <u>law</u> of the pendulum' and it was used to make clocks.

I left university in 1585 without a degree and began working as a teacher in mathematics. I also taught drawing to students at the Academy of the Arts of Drawing in Florence. By now, I loved 'the beauty of numbers'. I was also very interested in how the <u>weight</u> of an object could be <u>measured</u> using a <u>balance</u>. I <u>created</u> a thermoscope – an <u>instrument</u> which shows changes in <u>temperature</u>. This was later developed into the <u>thermometer</u>, which measured changes in temperature. In 1586, I wrote my first book. It described the design for a 'hydrostatic balance' – a <u>device</u> which weighed objects using air and water. I called the book *The Little Balance*.

Life was going well for me. But I wasn't earning a lot of money from private teaching. I needed to get a university job that paid a good salary. So I applied for teaching jobs at Sienna, Padua and Bologna universities. But I wasn't successful – probably because I didn't have a degree. Then, in 1589, I was offered the job of <u>Chair</u> of Mathematics at the University of Pisa.

At Pisa, I began to doubt Aristotle's <u>theories</u> about objects which fall. Aristotle – a Greek <u>philosopher</u> – believed that the weight of an object <u>decided</u> its speed when it fell. So I decided to carry out a simple experiment. I climbed to the top of the Leaning Tower of Pisa and I dropped balls of different weights to the ground. The balls were of different weights, but the same size. They all hit the ground at the same time. After this, I wrote my book called *On Motion*. In it, I said that the speed of objects which fall depends on their shape and size, not on their <u>weight</u> as Aristotle said. In the future, I said, a <u>theory</u> had to be tested before it was accepted.

◆ ◆ ◆

In 1591, my father died. I had to look after my brothers and sisters because I was the oldest child. This meant I needed to find work which paid a better salary. So from 1592 until 1610, I was Professor of Mathematics at Padua University. The job allowed me to teach, think and do many experiments.

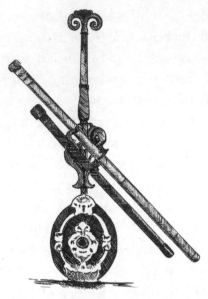

Galileo's telescope

During my time at Padua, I <u>invented</u> a water pump. I also invented a military compass — a device used by the army to plan battles. In 1609, the Italian scientist Paolo Sarpi wrote to me. He told me about a new <u>invention</u> in Holland called a 'telescope'. It was a device which magnified things — it made them look much bigger. The telescope allowed <u>astronomers</u> to look much more closely at the stars and planets in the sky. In a short time, I had developed its design. I called my telescope, 'Perspicullum'. Perspicullum could make the planets look eight times bigger than their normal size.

In 1610, I wrote a book called *Starry Messenger* about the discoveries that I'd made with my telescope. It described

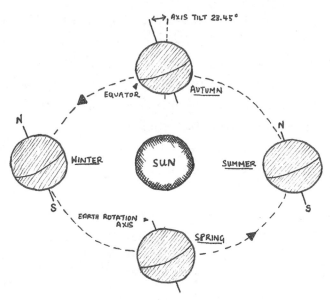

AXIS TILT 23.45°

EQUATOR

AUTUMN

N

WINTER

SUN

SUMMER

N

S

EARTH ROTATION AXIS

SPRING

S

Galileo believed that the Earth orbited the Sun

the mountains of the moon, as well as Jupiter's brightest four moons. In that same year, I also discovered the 'Phases of Venus' – the changes of Venus's light <u>caused</u> by the Sun. As I continued to use Perspicullum to study the planets, I began to ask questions about an important <u>religious</u> <u>belief</u>. In the 17th century, everyone believed the Earth was the centre of the universe. People thought that the planets and the Sun orbited around us. But my telescope showed me that the Earth and other planets orbited the Sun.

In 1611, I became Chief Mathematician at the University of Pisa. There, I wrote my *Discourse on Floating Bodies* and *Letters on <u>Sunspots</u>*. I also described my theories about the Earth and Sun to the Grand Duchess Christina of Tuscany. The letter was sent to Christina in 1615 but not published until 1636. When they read my letter, the priests of the <u>Catholic</u> Church in Rome became very angry. I agreed with the beliefs of the great mathematician and astronomer, Copernicus. Like Copernicus, I was asking questions about the belief that the Earth was the centre of the universe and not just a small part of it. My theories soon brought me terrible trouble.

In 1632, I published my book *Dialogue Concerning the Two Chief World Systems*. It had taken me six years to write it. But the book was <u>banned</u> by the <u>pope</u> as soon as it was published. All my other writings were banned, too. At first, I was <u>charged</u> with <u>heresy</u> and <u>sentenced</u> to death. Later this sentence was changed to <u>house arrest</u>.

I spent the rest of my life locked in my house. But I continued with my writing and experiments. In 1638, I wrote another book called *Discourses and Mathematical Demonstrations Concerning Two Sciences*. It was about my work in physics and my studies on <u>gravitation</u>. The book was banned in Italy but published later in Holland.

By now, I was getting old and I was often sick and in great pain. But I wasn't allowed to see doctors or take medicine. In 1636, I started to lose my eyesight. By the following year, I'd gone blind and I could not hear well. But my mind continued to work and my student, Vincenzo Viviani, became my eyes and ears. He carried out experiments for me and wrote down the results. In 1642, I died at my house in Arcetri, near Florence. I was 77 years old. I was kept under house arrest until the day I died.

The Life of Galileo Galilei

1564   Galileo Galilei was born in Pisa, Italy. He was the oldest of six children.

1572   When he was 8 years old, Galileo's family moved to Florence. However, Galileo stayed in Pisa, in the care of a relative.

1574   Galileo joined his family in Florence.

1575   Galileo attended the Camaldolese Monastery, at Vallombrosa, near Florence.

1581   He began studying medicine at the University of Pisa. He then changed his course to mathematics and philosophy.

1585   Galileo left Pisa University without a degree and worked as a teacher of mathematics.

1586   He published his book *The Little Balance*.

1588   He worked as a teacher at the Academy of the Arts of Drawing in Florence.

1589   Galileo became Professor of Mathematics at the University of Pisa.

1590   He wrote his book *On Motion*.

1591   His father died and Galileo had to look after his brothers and sisters.

1592–1610   Galileo was Professor of Mathematics at the University of Padua.

1595   He invented a compass.

1600   His book *Mechanics* was written.

1609   He improved the design of the telescope and called it 'Perspicullum'.

1610   Galileo published *Starry Messenger*. He looked at the mountains of the moon as well as Jupiter's brightest four moons. He discovered The Phases of Venus.

1611   He became Chief Mathematician at Padua University.

1612   Galileo wrote *Discourse on Floating Bodies*.

1613   He wrote *Letters on Sunspots*.

1615   His *Letter to Grand Duchess Christina* was written. However, it was not published until 1636.

1616   The Catholic Church became angry with his ideas. They warned him about his Copernican beliefs and banned his writings. Galileo wrote *Discourse on the Tides*.

1619   Galileo published *Discourse on the Comets*.

1623   *The Assayer* was published.

1632   He published *Dialogue Concerning the Two Chief World Systems.*

1633   Galileo was found guilty of heresy and sentenced to house arrest. The Catholic Church banned *Dialogue Concerning the Two Chief World Systems.*

1638   Galileo published *Dialogues Concerning Two New Sciences.*

1642   Galileo stayed under house arrest until his death. He died, aged 77, in his house at Arcetri near Florence in Italy.

René Descartes

◆ ◆ ◆

1596–1650

the man who said 'I think, therefore I am.'

I was a French <u>philosopher</u> and mathematician. I wanted to find the truth about <u>existence</u>. Many people disagreed with my work, but for me the truth was all that mattered.

◆ ◆ ◆

I was born in 1596 in La Haye en Touraine, in France (later they changed its name to Descartes, Indre-et-Loire). Unfortunately, my mother died the next year giving birth to my younger brother. My brother also died.

My father, Joachim Descartes, was a member of the <u>Parliament</u> of Brittany. Life for him was very hard after the death of his wife and son. It was difficult for him to work and look after me at the same time. So he sent me away to study at the Royal Henry-Le-Grand college, in Anjou.

Then I studied Law at the University of Poitiers. After <u>graduating</u>, I worked as a lawyer for a short time. But I wasn't happy being a lawyer. I didn't want to stay in one place. I wanted to learn about people and have many different experiences. So I decided to leave my job and go to Holland, where I joined the Dutch army. I spent the next ten years travelling as a soldier in Europe.

Then, in 1619, while I was with the army in Neuburg an der Donau, something amazing happened. On the nights of 10th and 11th November, I had three very strange dreams. In these dreams, ghosts came to me and showed me a new <u>philosophy</u>. They told me I had to look for truth and <u>reason</u> and I needed to study <u>logic</u> and science. After the dreams, the search for reason became my life's work.

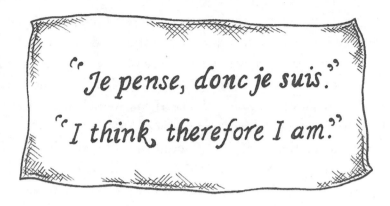

"Je pense, donc je suis."

"I think, therefore I am."

So I returned to France and <u>based</u> myself in Paris, although I continued to travel through Europe. While I was travelling, I began writing my first book. I called it *Rules for the Direction of the Mind*. The book prepared all my future work on mathematics, science and philosophy. In total, I had 36 rules in my mind, but I only managed to write down 21 of them during my life. I continued to travel and I experienced many things. During 1627, I saw the battle of La Rochelle. It was a terrible sight and many people were killed. The battle made me think about <u>religious</u> <u>beliefs</u>.

I became full of doubt about religious beliefs and, in 1628, I decided to move to Holland. It was my home for the next 21 years. In Holland, I joined the University of Franeker and I started working on my famous *Treatise on The World*. In the following year, I moved to Leiden University to study mathematics and <u>astronomy</u>.

Then, in 1633, I heard worrying news from Italy. The great mathematician Galileo had been <u>sentenced</u> to house arrest. The Catholic priests were unhappy because some of his theories had questioned their religious beliefs. When I heard this news, I became worried that the same thing could happen to me. As a result, I decided not to publish my essay *Treatise on The World*, which was about how to discover the truth in science.

I believed that science was about thought, and learning from our experiences. In 1637, I published part of my *Treatise on The World* in three essays: *Optics, Geometry,* and *Meteorology*. The essays began with my famous *Discourse on the Method*. I wrote about the belief that the mind is separate from the body. This belief is now called 'Cartesianism'. I decided to ask a simple question – 'How do we know we exist?' And my famous answer was, 'I think, therefore I am'.

♦ ◆ ♦

I wanted to understand more about life. So I moved from place to place. I lived in Dordrecht, Amsterdam, Utrecht and many other towns and cities in Holland. During this time, I decided to change my name to 'Poitevin' – 'someone who comes from the town of Poitiers'. I wanted to create a new identity for myself. 'Poitevin' was able to meet many new and interesting people.

I wrote my most famous work during my time in Holland. I called it *Meditations on First Philosophy*. It was a work which changed mathematical and philosophical ideas. Unfortunately, academics at Leiden and Utrecht

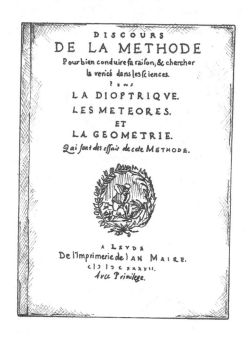

did not like the book. They'd begun to <u>criticize</u> my ideas. As a result I became very worried. I didn't want to be arrested like Galileo!

Fortunately, I knew some very important people in Europe and they helped to protect me. In 1643 I began to exchange letters with Princess Elizabeth of Bohemia. Elizabeth was very intelligent and she spoke six languages. I wrote my *Passions of the Soul* for the Princess in 1649. In 1647, the King of France gave me a pension – a salary for the rest of my life. I was happy that the importance of my work had finally been realized and understood by my home country. I continued to write and teach and in 1649, I travelled to Stockholm to teach Queen Christina of Sweden. But the weather in Sweden was cold and wet and it made my health bad. After a short time, I became ill.

On 11th February 1650, I died. The doctors said I died from a fever. But other people thought I was murdered because the pope – the leader of the Catholic Church – did not agree with my theories. Thirteen years after my death, the Catholic Church banned all my books.

I had always believed in God, but I also wanted to study the truth and reason. For me, it was possible to do both things.

The Life of René Descartes

1596   René Descartes was born in La Haye en Touraine (now called Descartes, Indre-et-Loire) in France.

1597   René's mother died giving birth to another son, who also died.

1604   At the age of eight, René entered the Royal Henry-Le-Grand college at La Flèche in Anjou.

1616   René continued his education at the University of Poitiers, where he studied Law.

1618   He moved to Holland and joined the Dutch army. René travelled for ten years through Europe as a soldier.

1619   René had three dreams while he was with the army in Neuburg an der Donau. He dreamed he had to look for truth and reason. He began writing *Rules for the Direction of the Mind*. It was not published until 1684.

1622   René returned home to France. He based himself in Paris, but he continued to travel in Europe.

1627   René saw the battle of La Rochelle.

1628   He continued to write *Rules for the Direction of Mind*. In the same year he returned to Holland. It was his home for the next 21 years.

1629–1630   René began working on his *Treatise of The World*. He joined the University of Franeker. In 1630, he began to use the name 'Poitevin' and joined the Leiden University to study mathematics and astronomy.

1633   He decided not to publish *Treatise of The World* after the arrest of Galileo.

1637   At the age of 41, René published *Discourse on the Method, Optics, Geometry, and Meteorology*.

1641   He published *Meditations on First Philosophy*.

1643   René began to exchange letters with Princess Elisabeth of Bohemia.

1644   He visited France and published *The Principles of Philosophy*.

1647   René was given a pension by the King of France. He published *Comments on a Certain Broadsheet* and began work on *The Description of the Human Body*.

1649   He moved to Sweden to teach Queen
       Christina. In the same year, he published
       Passions of the Soul.

1650   René died aged 53 in Stockholm, Sweden.
       Some people thought that he was murdered.

Isaac Newton

◆ ◆ ◆

1643–1727

the man who watched an apple fall from a tree

I was the man who watched an apple fall to the ground and discovered the <u>laws</u> of <u>gravity</u>. People today say I was one of the most important scientists who ever lived.

◆ ◆ ◆

I was born on 25th December in 1643 in a small village in Lincolnshire, England. I was given the same name as my father, Isaac Newton, a wealthy farmer who'd died three months before my birth. When I was 3 years old, my mother married again and went to live with her husband. I stayed with my grandmother on my father's farm. But in 1653, my mother's new husband died and she returned to our village with their three children (my half-brother and two half-sisters).

In 1654, I started attending The King's School in the town of Grantham which was nearby. But it was not a very happy time for me. My teachers said I was lazy and told me that I didn't listen. But I wasn't happy with the way they were teaching me. I could not learn just by repeating facts and I'd become very bored. When I was 17 years old, I decided to leave school. My mother owned a farm and she wanted me to become a farmer – but I hated farming. Later, the headmaster of the King's School Henry Stokes, asked me to finish my education. I agreed and returned to school. This time I became the school's top student.

In June 1661, I became a student of Law at Trinity College, Cambridge. I studied the ideas of Aristotle there, as well as the ideas of Copernicus and Kepler. In 1665, I graduated with a Bachelor of Arts degree. But in the same year, the plague – a terrible illness which killed many people – arrived, and the university had to close for two years. I continued my studies in Grantham. I'd become very interested in the subjects of calculus and optics, and in the laws of gravitation. During my time as a student at Cambridge, I studied the ideas and philosophy of René Descartes. I had read his *Géométrie* and other books.

I also became interested in Galileo and in his work on the laws of motion, or movement. Galileo had always believed that tides – the rise and fall of the sea – were caused by the Sun. But I'd started to believe that tides were caused by the gravitational pull of the Moon.

In 1667, I returned to Cambridge as a Fellow (a senior member) of Trinity College. During my time in Grantham, I'd started to think more about truth and fact. I wondered if I could find them using mathematical calculations. As a result, I began writing a book about calculus called *The Method of Fluxions and Infinite Series*. It was published 65 years later.

In 1668, I developed Galileo's design for a telescope – a device which makes things look bigger. Many people could use my new design.

And in the next year, I became Professor of Mathematics at Cambridge University. That was my job for the next 34 years. During my time at Cambridge, I studied many scientific subjects. For example, from 1670 to 1672, I concentrated on optics and the subject of light. My experiments showed me that light was a collection of many colours. This became a subject of great interest to me over the next 30 years. My book *Opticks*, which was published much later, in 1704, explained my theories about light.

In 1672, I was elected as a Fellow of the Royal Society and my work on light and colours was published in the Society's journal. My work was becoming famous. But other academics criticized me and my work. In 1678, the philosopher, Robert Hooke, criticized some of my ideas about light. After this, I became depressed and I couldn't sleep. It became difficult for me to leave my house and I didn't want to see anyone. But I continued my studies at

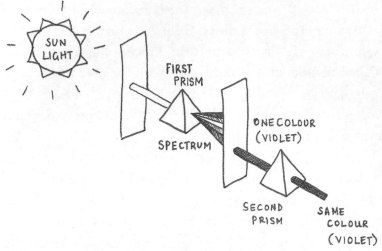

SUN LIGHT

FIRST PRISM

SPECTRUM

ONE COLOUR (VIOLET)

SECOND PRISM

SAME COLOUR (VIOLET)

Newton experimented in optics and light

home. I studied physics and the movement of the planets. During this time, I developed my <u>theory</u> of universal gravitation. I was now sure that gravity was the <u>reason</u> for tides – the rise and fall of the sea. I also thought about the changing of the seasons.

In 1687, I described these theories in my most famous work, *Principia*. Some academics have called it 'the greatest scientific book ever written'. But I replied that I had 'stood on the shoulders of giants' – or great men. I meant that most of the work had already been done before me by men like Descartes and Galileo.

In 1689, I was elected to the <u>Parliament</u> of England. In the two years between 1689 and 1690, I argued that all political laws should be <u>based</u> on scientific fact, not <u>religious</u> belief. As a result, a new law was <u>created</u> which took power from the King and gave it to Parliament. However, I didn't enjoy political work. In Parliament, I noticed that reason and fact were not very important. It was always the politicians with the loudest voices who won the arguments.

In 1696, I was given the job of Warden of the Royal Mint – I had to <u>measure</u> and control England's money. The job gave me the chance to use my mathematical theory. I had to decide how much money should be in <u>circulation</u>. In 1699, I was promoted to Master of the Mint and that was my job until I died.

In 1703, I was elected as President of the Royal Society. And in 1705, Queen Anne came to Trinity College to make me a Knight of the Realm. At the age of 62, I had become *Sir* Isaac Newton. In my final years, I moved to Kensington, near London, and was looked after by my niece. On 31st March 1727, I died in my sleep. My body was buried in Westminster Abbey in London.

The Life of Isaac Newton

1643   Isaac Newton was born in the village
of Woolsthorpe-by-Colsterworth,
Lincolnshire, England. He was given the
same name as his father, who had died
three months earlier.

1646   When he was 3 years old, his mother
married again and moved to live with her
new husband. Isaac was left in the care of
his grandmother.

1653   His mother's husband died and she returned
with her three new children to live with him.

1654   Isaac attended Grantham Grammar School.

1661   He became a student at Trinity College,
Cambridge University and studied Law.

1665   After he graduated with a Bachelor of Arts
degree, the University closed because of the
plague. Isaac went home and continued to
study mathematics, physics and astronomy.

1666   Isaac became interested in calculus, optics
and gravity.

1667   He returned to the University as a fellow of
Trinity College.

1668   Isaac developed Galileo's telescope design so that other people could use it. He also received his Master of Arts degree.

1669   He became Professor of Mathematics at Trinity College. It was his job for the next 34 years.

1670–1672   He concentrated his studies on optics.

1671   Isaac finished his book *The Method of Fluxions and Infinite Series*, which was not published until 1736.

1672   He was elected as a Fellow of the Royal Society. His theory about light and colours was published in the Royal Society's journal.

1687   Isaac published *Philosophiae Naturalis Principa Mathematica* – the *Principia*. It was published in three sections. It is one of the most important scientific works in history.

1689   He was elected to the Parliament of England.

1696   He moved to London and was given the job of Warden of the Royal Mint.

1699   Isaac was promoted to Master of the Mint. It was his job for the rest of his life.

1701   Between 1701 and 1725, Isaac wrote several reports as Master of the Mint. He was elected for a second time to the Parliament of England. He left his job as Professor of Mathematics at Cambridge.

1703   He was elected as President of the Royal Society.

1704   He published *Opticks*.

1705   He was knighted by Queen Anne and became *Sir* Isaac Newton.

1707   His mathematics text *Arithmetica Universalis* was published.

1725   When his health began to fail, he moved to Kensington, near London.

1727   Isaac died in his sleep, aged 84.

Carl Friedrich Gauss

♦ ♦ ♦

1777–1855

the man who is called 'The Prince of Mathematicians'

As a child, I was better at mathematics than my teachers. I helped develop many scientific and mathematical subjects and I'm known today as 'The Prince of Mathematicians'.

◆ ◆ ◆

I was born in Brunswick in Germany, in 1777. When I was a child, I was a <u>genius</u> at mathematics. My father told me that I could add up numbers by the age of 3. At primary school, my teachers gave me a test. 'Add up the numbers from 1 to 100 in order,' they said. I gave them the correct answer in a few seconds. My mathematical ability was surprising because both my parents were poor and they didn't go to school. My father was a builder and gardener, and my mother could not read or write. They wanted me to become a farmer after I finished school.

But my teachers noticed my ability and they wanted me to continue my studies. So at the age of 13, I started attending Brunswick's Gymnasium school. During this time, Charles Ferdinand, the Duke of Brunswick, learned of my genius with numbers. In 1792, he paid for me to study at a special school called the Brunswick Collegium Carolinum. I studied <u>astronomy</u>, maths and geography there.

In 1795, I became a student at the University of Göttingen, in the part of Germany called Lower Saxony. In my first year, I did a lot of work on <u>geometry</u> and advanced mathematics. At the age of 18, I became the first person to prove a difficult <u>theory</u>. Mathematicians today call this theory 'the <u>law</u> of quadratic reciprocity'. The study of 'prime numbers' also greatly interested me – a prime number can only be divided by one or itself.

In 1799, after four years of study, I left university without a degree. Fortunately the Duke of Brunswick continued to pay for my <u>academic</u> research. In the same year, I began writing a textbook called *Disquisitiones Arithmeticae*. The book was a discussion of <u>algebra</u> and the connection of algebra to <u>geometric</u> shapes.

My academic life with numbers was a quiet one, but the world around me was filled with trouble. In France, there had been a terrible <u>revolution</u> and many people had been killed. America had just fought a war against England. In Europe, Napoleon was preparing for war.

But I tried not to think about what was happening and spent my time studying and working.

In late 1800, a small planet called Ceres was discovered by the <u>astronomer</u> Giuseppe Piazzi. However, during the next year it disappeared behind the sun. I was one of three experts who were asked to <u>calculate</u> its position. The work took me three months to complete. Then, in December of that year, Ceres was seen again. The other two experts had been wrong, but I had correctly calculated the planet's new position! My work on Ceres gave me an interest in astronomy. I wanted to develop methods to calculate the positions of our planets. Of course, I understood we couldn't control our universe, but we could still study and <u>measure</u> it. My <u>astronomical</u> work <u>inspired</u> me to look at other problems of <u>measurement</u>. As a result, I wrote about my method of reducing mistakes (or errors, as they are called in the world of science) when measuring distances. I'd used this method when I found the position of the planet Ceres.

◆ ◆ ◆

As a result of this important work I was made a Fellow (a member) of the <u>Royal Society</u> of London. Then, in 1807, I was given the job of Professor of Mathematics at Göttingen University. I was also made Director of its Observatory. I worked at the Göttingen Observatory for the rest of my life.

Things were going well in my life, but difficult times were ahead. In 1805, I had fallen in love with, and married, Johanna Osthoff. Together, we had three children. Then in 1809, Johanna died giving birth to our second son. The boy died soon after Johanna. In the months that followed, I became very depressed.

The next year, I married Minna Waldeck – Johanna's best friend. We had three children, who all <u>survived</u>. But Minna was always more like a friend to me than a wife. It was Johanna who I had really loved. Many people said that I never recovered from her death.

In 1818, I was asked to <u>survey</u> the Kingdom of Hanover. It was an important job and I spent many months riding a horse across the land. Surveying the land interested me and it <u>led to</u> a theory in geometry called 'Gaussian curvature'. To help my work, I <u>invented</u> a heliotrope – an <u>instrument</u> that uses mirrors and the Sun to measure distances.

◆ ◆ ◆

In 1831, Minna died after a long illness. My mother, who had also been ill for a long time, died eight years later, in 1839. It was a difficult time in my life. I was very unhappy, but I continued to work and study hard. During this time, I met the scientist Wilhelm Weber. Together, we used what we knew about electricity and <u>magnetism</u> to <u>create</u> a telegraph <u>device</u>. The <u>instrument</u> could send messages (they were later called 'telegraphs')

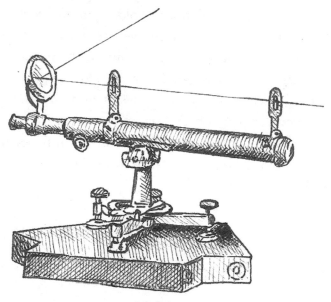

A heliotrope

over a distance of 15,000 metres. Unfortunately, the Göttingen Observatory did not want to <u>invest</u> money in our <u>invention</u>. Many years later, the device was developed into the electronic telegraph machine.

In 1838, I received the Royal Society's Copley Medal – a prize given for important achievements in science. In 1840, I published my famous *Dioptrische Untersuchungen* which led to a difficult mathematical <u>calculation</u> called the 'Gaussian lens formula'. I never published my theories quickly – I always wanted to prove them first. Most people used intelligent guesses <u>based</u> on their experience. But I believed it was possible, with the correct information, to <u>decide</u> <u>probability</u>.

In 1849, I gave my famous 'Golden Jubilee' lecture to an audience of scientists and mathematicians. As a result, I received many kind messages from <u>academics</u> all over Europe. In my life I'd greatly developed the subjects of mathematics, astronomy and physics and my methods became very important for surveying and measuring. In the years that followed my lecture, my health began to suffer. In 1855, I died in my sleep in Göttingen. I was 77 years old.

The Life of Carl Friedrich Gauss

1777   Carl Friedrich Gauss was born in
                Brunswick, Lower Saxony, Germany.

1780–1791   His genius for numbers was noticed by his
                teachers and Charles Ferdinand, the Duke
                of Brunswick.

1792   The Duke of Brunswick paid for Carl to go
                to the Collegium Carolinum.

1795   He went on to study at the University of
                Göttingen where he did important work
                on geometry and the theory of 'quadratic
                reciprocity law'. He also became interested
                in prime numbers.

1799   He left university without a degree. In the
                same year he started writing *Disquisitiones
                Arithmeticae*. The book was a discussion of
                algebra.

1801   He published *Disquisitiones Arithmeticae* and
                found the position of the planet Ceres.

1804–1805   He was made a Fellow of the Royal Society
                of London. Carl married his first wife,
                Johanna Osthoff, and they later had three
                children.

1807	Carl was given the job of Professor at Göttingen University and Director of the Göttingen Observatory.
1809	His wife, Johanna, died giving birth to their second son. Their son died soon after.
1810	Carl married Johanna's best friend, Minna Waldeck, and they had three children. He published the *Theoria Motus Corporum Coelestium in Sectionibus Conicis Solem Ambientium*.
1818–1832	Carl began measuring the land of Hanover. The work led to Carl's invention of the heliotrope.
1820	Carl became a Fellow of the Royal Society, Edinburgh.
1831	His second wife died.
1833	He worked with Wilhelm Weber. They invented the telegraph device, which could send messages over a distance of 15,000 metres.
1838	He received the Royal Society of London's Copley Medal.
1839	His mother died after a long illness.

1840   He published *Dioptrische Untersuchungen* which led to a calculation called the 'Gaussian lens formula'.

1849   He gave his Golden Jubilee lecture to an audience of mathematicians. As a result, he received kind messages from academics all over Europe.

1855   Carl Gauss died, aged 77, in Göttingen.

Charles Babbage

♦ ♦ ♦

1791–1871

the man who invented computers

Next time you use the Internet or send an email, you can think of me. My <u>invention</u>, the 'Analytical Engine', was the first computer. You can see it today at the Science Museum in London.

◆ ◆ ◆

I was born on 26th December 1791, in London, England. My father, Benjamin Babbage, was a banker. My childhood wasn't a happy one. When I was 8 years old, I became ill with a fever. I was sent away from London to recover at a school in Devon. After that, I attended the King Edward the Sixth Grammar school in Totnes for a short time. However, I was taught at home for most of my childhood because of my poor health.

One of my teachers gave me books to read by some well-known living mathematicians. In 1810, I went to study at Trinity College, Cambridge, and I realized that I knew more about modern mathematical <u>theory</u> than my teachers. They were still teaching <u>calculus</u> developed by Newton! As a result, I <u>created</u> 'The Analytical Society' with my friends, George Peacock and John Herschel. The society's purpose was to improve the teaching of mathematics at Cambridge.

I changed my course and moved from Trinity to Peterhouse College, where I became its top student. I married Georgiana Whitmore in the year that I <u>graduated</u>. But my father was not happy about the marriage. He said that I was too young and I could not afford to have a wife and children. After our wedding, Georgiana and I moved to Marylebone in London. We had eight children, but unfortunately only four of them <u>survived</u>.

My <u>academic</u> career began well. In 1815, I lectured at the <u>Royal Institution</u> on <u>astronomy</u> and I was <u>elected</u> a Fellow (a member) of the <u>Royal Society</u> the following year. But during this time, my father had to give me money to help my family. This made me very unhappy. I needed to earn more money so I tried to find a teaching job at a university. I applied for many jobs, but I wasn't successful.

In 1820, I helped to create the <u>Astronomical</u> Society, which later became the Royal Astronomical Society. Our plan was to make astronomical <u>calculations</u> simpler and to share data – information – more easily. As a result, I began developing my idea for a 'Difference Engine' – the first machine which could make and print mathematical calculations. By 1822, the engine was working. It was eight feet tall, weighed about 15 tons, and it had about 25,000 parts. In 1824, I received the Royal Astronomical Society's Gold Medal. This was a special prize given to me for my work on the Difference Engine. Two years later I published *A Comparative View of the Different Institutions for the Assurance of Life* and the following year I produced a table of logarithms from 1 to 1,008,000.

Things were going very well. But then, in 1827, my wife suddenly died. My father and my two sons also died a short time later. It was a terrible time and I became very depressed. I felt that I had no reason to live. My friends told me to go abroad and rest. I took their advice and spent some time travelling through Europe. I was staying in Rome when I heard some wonderful news. I had been offered the job of Lucasian Professor of Mathematics at Cambridge.

I quickly accepted the job and returned to England. There, I continued to develop my Difference Engine. I made a new machine which I called the 'Analytical Engine'. The Analytical Engine was the first design like a modern computer and it used punchcards to control a calculator. It was launched in 1834 with an investment of £17,000 from the government. I also invested £6,000. However, after eight years, the government said my invention was 'worthless' – it had no value. The politicians and scientists couldn't understand that I had made a great breakthrough. So I decided the answer was to become a politician myself. In 1832 and 1834, I tried to be elected to <u>Parliament</u>. But I wasn't successful.

◆ ◆ ◆

I continued with my work and in 1834, I started the <u>Statistical</u> Society of London – a society for <u>statisticians</u>. I met many interesting people because of that organization. One of these people was a very intelligent woman called Ada Lovelace. Ada was the daughter of the famous poet, Lord Byron, but her talent was with mathematics, not words. Ada was very interested in the Analytical Engine. She understood how important it was. She helped me to make notes about my work and she used an <u>algorithm</u> to create the first computer program. Ada believed that my machine was very important for the future – for the <u>production</u> of books, pictures and music.

Other people also became interested in the Analytical Engine. In 1854, the Swedish <u>inventor</u>, Georg Scheutz, started to develop my design. But unfortunately, there wasn't much interest in my work during my life. I wasn't good at talking to politicians and they didn't understand the importance of my inventions. As a result, the first useful computers weren't built until the 1940s.

While I was working on the Analytical Engine, I wrote many books. *Reflections on the Decline of Science in England* was published in 1830. *On the Economy of Machinery and Manufactures* followed in 1832. Later, I wrote *The Exposition of 1851* and my main thoughts were in my last book, *Passages*

from the Life of a Philosopher, published in 1864. All these works were about the progress of my theories and inventions and about many scientific and mathematical subjects.

During my life I <u>invented</u> many things. But most people remember me because of my work on computers. Today, most people have a computer and millions of emails are sent every day. Computers have changed business and daily life. They have also changed the production of films, music and books – Ada Lovelace was right.

In the later years of my life, I left my job as Professor at Cambridge and I lost interest in politics. I concentrated on my studies of <u>measurement</u> and computer calculation.

On 18th October 1871, I died peacefully at my home in Marylebone, where I had lived for 40 years. I was 79 years old.

The Life of Charles Babbage

1791   Charles Babbage was born in London, England.

1799–1809   When he was 8 years old, he became ill. He was sent to a school in the countryside in Devon to recover. He later attended King Edward the Sixth Grammar School in Totnes for a short time.

1810   Charles went to Trinity College, Cambridge, and later moved to Peterhouse College.

1812   He started the Analytical Society with John Herschel, George Peacock and others.

1814   Charles graduated from Cambridge. He married Georgiana Whitmore and they had eight children. However, only four of their children survived.

1815   He lectured on astronomy at the Royal Institution.

1816   He was elected a Fellow of the Royal Society.

1820   He helped to start the Astronomical Society.

1822 Charles started work on the 'Difference Engine'. He began to develop his machine with money from the British Government in the following year. He published *Observations on the Application of Machinery to the Computation of Mathematical Tables* and *On the Theoretical Principles of Machinery for Calculating Tables*, in Brewster's *Journal of Science*.

1824 He won the Gold Medal of the Royal Astronomical Society.

1826 Charles published *A Comparative View of the Different Institutions for the Assurance of Life*.

1827 He published his table of logarithms from 1 to 1,008,000. Charles's father, his wife, and two of his sons died. He took some holiday from work and travelled throughout Europe.

1828 He became Lucasian Professor of Mathematics at Cambridge. Charles stayed in the job until 1839.

1830 He published *Reflections on the Decline of Science in England: and on Some of its Causes*.

1831 Charles started the British Association for the Advancement of Science.

1832 He published *On the Economy of Machinery and Manufactures*. Charles tried to be elected to Parliament, but was not successful.

1834   Charles helped to start the Statistical Society
        for London. The Analytical Engine was
        launched, although it was never completed.
        He tried to enter Parliament again, but
        again was not successful. He met Ada
        Lovelace.

1838   He invented the dynamometer car.

1842   Ada Lovelace translated an article by Luigi
        Menabrea, on Charles's Analytical Engine.
        She later wrote a computer program using
        his notes.

1851   Charles published *The Exposition of 1851
        or, Views of the Industry, the Science, and the
        Government of England*.

1856   The design of the Analytical Engine was
        completed.

1864   Charles published *Passages from the Life of a
        Philosopher*.

1871   Charles died, aged 79, in London, England.

Ada Lovelace

◆ ◆ ◆

1815–1852

the woman who wrote the first computer program

My father was a famous poet, but I became
a brilliant mathematician. I worked with
Charles Babbage and helped him to develop
the Analytical Engine. People today call me
'the world's first computer programmer'.

♦ ◆ ♦

I was born in 1815, in London, England. My father was
the famous poet, Lord Byron, and my mother was Lady
Annabella Milbanke – or Lady Byron. Unfortunately, my
father died when I was only 8 years old. My mother and I
lived with her parents – my grandparents. Women didn't
usually get an education at that time and they didn't go to
school. But my mother, who was also very good at maths,
wanted me to have an education. She arranged for me to
have private lessons with a teacher.

It was good that my mother wanted me to have an education. However, she had very clear ideas about what was good for my mind. She didn't want me to study the <u>arts</u> because she didn't want me to be like my father. She wanted me to study mathematics and scientific subjects. I had many excellent teachers. They included William Frend, Augustus De Morgan and the science writer, Mary Somerville. I also studied very hard – some of my mother's friends thought that I worked *too* hard.

When I was 14 years old, I became ill. For a long time, I couldn't walk or move my body and I had to stay in bed for more than a year. But I continued to study many subjects. I was taught music and I became a very good musician. I also learned many languages. But mathematics was always my best subject. I thought numbers were beautiful and I became very interested in mathematical and scientific developments at that time. My scientific abilities became clear when, in 1828, I drew a design for a flying machine.

During this time, I read and enjoyed Mary Somerville's book, *The Mechanism of the Heavens*. It was about developments in mathematical <u>astronomy</u>. Mary and I became good friends and in 1834, she introduced me to the scientist William, Lord King. William was ten years older than me.

Mary also introduced me to the work of Charles Babbage, who at that time was Lucasian Professor of mathematics at Cambridge. I learned that Babbage was working on a <u>device</u> called the 'Difference Engine' – a machine that could make mathematical <u>calculations</u>.

When I was 18, Babbage and I were introduced at a society called the <u>Statistical</u> Society. He explained that he was developing the Difference Engine into a new machine called the Analytical Engine. Babbage's ideas were new and exciting and they made me think about the changing future of mathematics.

◆ ◆ ◆

When I was 19, in 1835, William, Lord King and I got married and later we had three children.

In 1838, William was given the title 'Earl Lovelace'. People called me, 'The Countess of Lovelace'. As a result of my marriage and my friendship with Mary Somerville, I met some very important people. I was introduced to the <u>inventor</u>, David Brewster, and to Charles Dickens, the famous writer. I also met the famous scientists Charles Wheatstone and Michael Faraday. They came to our house for dinner and spent the evening discussing their ideas with me.

Charles Babbage and I had the same interests and I understood his work better than most people. We began to exchange letters and share our ideas. In 1842, Charles went to Turin in Italy, and he gave a lecture on his work. The famous Italian mathematician, Luigi Menabrea, was there and he published an article on the most important parts of Babbage's speech. My Italian was very good,

so I offered to translate Menabrea's article into English. Charles was happy for me to do this. He also asked me to add my own notes to the translation. It took me nine months to write down all my ideas. The final document was three times longer than Menabrea's article!

Charles Babbage was very happy with the article and he decided to publish it. As a result, it appeared in Richard Taylor's *Scientific Memoirs* in 1843.

At the time, the politicians did not believe in Babbage's work and they did not want to <u>invest</u> a lot of money in it. They could not understand that he had made a very important <u>breakthrough</u>. Babbage never wrote articles and he preferred to show people his ideas and designs. I preferred to write things down. So together we made a very good team.

I wanted people to understand Charles Babbage's work and how important it was. I believed that his machine was important for the future – for science and other important purposes. People could use it for artistic purposes too – and for writing music and drawing pictures. In my notes, I worked out an <u>algorithm</u> to <u>calculate</u> a group of numbers called 'Bernoulli's numbers'. It was the first time an algorithm had been used with a computer. The 'Analytical Engine' is now seen as an early model for a computer and my notes were a description of its software. People today understand that they were the world's first computer program! We did not know it then, but we were <u>causing</u> the beginnings of the digital age.

◆ ◆ ◆

People now think of me as the first writer of computer software. But I was interested in many scientific subjects. In 1844, I visited the English electrical engineer Andrew Crosse to learn how to <u>carry out</u> electrical experiments. After this I wrote a paper called *Researches on Magnetism*. Unfortunately, it was never published. I also became very interested in the brain and how it <u>creates</u> feelings in human beings.

Unfortunately, I was not able to develop these interests. In 1852, problems with my health returned and I found out that I had cancer. I cried as I said goodbye to my children and husband and I asked to be buried next to my father. I died in the November of the same year, in Marylebone, London. I was only 36 years old.

The Life of Ada Lovelace

1815   Augusta Ada Byron was born in London, England. Her father was the poet, Lord Byron. Her mother was Anne Isabella 'Annabella' Milbanke (Lady Byron).

1824   Lord Byron died in Greece when Ada was 8 years old.

1828   Ada was taught at home. Her mathematical ability became obvious when she created the design for a flying machine.

1829   Ada became ill. She stayed in her bed for over a year but she continued her studies during that time.

1832   Ada's teachers realized that she was a very good mathematician. Ada's private teachers included the mathematician Augustus De Morgan, and the science writer Mary Somerville.

1833–1834   Mary introduced Ada to Charles Babbage and Ada began to study the 'Analytical Engine'. Babbage's ideas were new and exciting and they made her think about the changing future of mathematics. Mary also introduced Ada to the scientist William, Lord King.

1835   Ada became Baroness King when she
        married William, Lord King, 8th Baron
        King. They later had three children.

1838   William became the Earl of Lovelace and
        Ada became The Countess of Lovelace.

1842   Ada translated an article written about
        Charles Babbage's Analytical Engine and
        added her own notes.

1843   Her translated article appeared in Richard
        Taylor's *Scientific Memoirs*. People now
        understand that she had written the world's
        first computer program.

1844   Ada visited the electrical engineer Andrew
        Crosse to learn how to carry out electrical
        experiments. She wrote a review of a paper
        by Baron Karl von Reichenbach, *Researches
        on Magnetism,* but this was not published.

1852   Ada died aged 36, in Marylebone, London.
        She asked to be buried next to her father.

academic NOUN
a member of a university or college who teaches or does research

ADJECTIVE
relating to the work done in schools, universities and colleges

algebra NOUN
a type of mathematics in which letters and signs are used to represent numbers

algorithm NOUN
a series of mathematical steps, especially in a computer program, which will give you the answer to a particular kind of problem or question

arts NOUN
activities such as music, painting, literature, film, theatre and dance

astronomer NOUN
a scientist who studies the stars, planets and other natural objects in space

astronomical ADJECTIVE
relating to the study of stars, planets and other natural objects in space

astronomy NOUN
the scientific study of the stars, planets and other natural objects in space

balance NOUN
a device for weighing things. It has a bar with a known weight on one end and an object you want to weigh on the other end. You keep changing the known weight until the bar is level, which then tells you the weight of your object.

ban VERB
to say officially that something must not be done, shown or used

base VERB
1 to have somewhere as the main place where you work, stay or live

2 to develop something such as an idea from something else

belief NOUN
1 a religious or political view

2 a feeling of being certain that something is real or true

breakthrough NOUN
an important discovery that is made after a lot of hard work

calculate VERB
to discover something such as the amount or position of something, using mathematics

calculation NOUN
a way of discovering something such as an amount using mathematics

calculus NOUN
a branch of advanced mathematics that deals with variable quantities

carry out VERB
to do something

Catholic ADJECTIVE
belonging to the Christian Church that has the pope as its leader

cause VERB
to make something happen

Chair NOUN
the post of professor at a university

charge VERB
to formally accuse someone of committing a crime

circulation NOUN
the fact that something such as money is being used by the public

create VERB
to make something happen or exist

criticize VERB
to express your disapproval of someone or something

decide VERB
to cause a particular result

device NOUN
something that has been invented for a particular purpose

elect VERB
to choose a person to do a particular job by voting for them

exist VERB
to be a real thing or situation, or to really be alive

existence NOUN
the fact that something is a real thing or situation or that someone is really alive

genius NOUN
a very skilled or intelligent person

geometric ADJECTIVE
consisting of regular shapes or lines

geometry NOUN
a type of mathematics relating to lines, angles, curves and shapes

graduate VERB
to complete your studies at college or university

gravitation NOUN
the force that causes objects to be attracted towards each other because they have mass

gravitational ADJECTIVE
causing objects to be attracted towards each other because they have mass

gravity NOUN
the force that makes things fall to the ground

heresy NOUN
a belief or way of behaving that disagrees with accepted religious beliefs

heretic NOUN
someone whose beliefs or actions are considered wrong because they disagree with accepted religious beliefs

house arrest NOUN
a situation in which someone is not allowed to leave their home, because they are suspected of illegal activity

identity NOUN
your name and who you are

inspire VERB
to give you new ideas and a strong feeling of enthusiasm

instrument NOUN
a piece of scientific equipment that is used for measuring things such as weight, heat or speed

invent VERB
to be the first person to think of something or to make it

invention NOUN
something that has been invented by someone

inventor NOUN
a person who has invented something, or whose job is to invent things

invest VERB
to put money into a business or a bank, in order to try to make a profit from it

investment NOUN
an amount of money that someone puts into a business or a bank

journal NOUN
a magazine or a newspaper that deals with a special subject

launch VERB
to start a large and important activity

law NOUN
a scientific rule that someone has invented to explain a particular natural process

lead to VERB
to cause a particular situation

logarithm NOUN
a number that can represent another number in order to make a difficult multiplication or division sum simpler

logic NOUN
a way of working things out, by saying that one fact must be true if another fact is true

magnetism NOUN
the natural power of some objects and substances, especially iron, to attract other objects towards them

measure VERB
to find out the size or amount of something

measurement NOUN
the process of measuring something in order to find its size or amount

movement NOUN
the fact that something changes its position

optics NOUN
the branch of science concerned with vision, sight and light

orbit VERB
to move regularly around a planet, a moon or the sun

Parliament NOUN
the group of people who make or change the laws of some countries or regions

pendulum NOUN
a rod with a weight at the end which swings from side to side in a regular way

philosopher NOUN
a person who studies or writes about philosophy

philosophy NOUN
the study of ideas about the meaning of life, knowledge and reality

pope NOUN
the head of the Roman Catholic Church

probability NOUN
the part of mathematics that deals with how likely something is to happen

production NOUN
the process of making or creating
something

punchcard NOUN
a card with holes in a particular
pattern, used in the past to
program computers

reason NOUN
1 the ability that people have to
think and to make sensible
judgments
2 a fact or situation that causes
something to happen or explains
why it happens

religious ADJECTIVE
connected with religion

revolution NOUN
an attempt by a group of people
to change their country's
government by using force

Royal Institution NOUN
an organization formed in 1799
in Britain to promote scientific
knowledge

Royal Society NOUN
an organization formed in 1662
in Britain to promote scientific
knowledge

sentence VERB
to give someone a particular
punishment for committing
a crime

statistical ADJECTIVE
relating to the use or study of
statistics

statistician NOUN
a person who studies statistics
(= facts that are expressed in
numbers) or who works using
statistics

sunspot NOUN
one of the dark cool patches that
appear on the surface of the sun
and last for about a week

survey VERB
to examine and measure an area
of land, usually in order to make a
map of it

survive VERB
to continue to live, especially
after a difficult or dangerous time

temperature NOUN
a measure of how hot or cold
something is

theory NOUN
an idea or a set of ideas that tries
to explain something

thermometer NOUN
an instrument for measuring how
hot or cold something is

weight NOUN
how heavy something is

Collins
English Readers

AMAZING PEOPLE READERS AT OTHER LEVELS:

Level 1

Amazing Inventors
978-0-00-754494-3

Amazing Women
978-0-00-754493-6

Amazing Leaders
978-0-00-754492-9

Amazing Performers
978-0-00-754508-7

**Amazing Entrepreneurs and
Business People**
978-0-00-754501-8

Level 3

Amazing Explorers
978-0-00-754497-4

Amazing Performers
978-0-00-754505-6

Amazing Writers
978-0-00-754498-1

Amazing Scientists
978-0-00-754510-0

Amazing Philanthropists
978-0-00-754504-9

Level 4

**Amazing Thinkers and
Humanitarians**
978-0-00-754499-8

Amazing Leaders
978-0-00-754507-0

**Amazing Entrepreneurs and
Business People**
978-0-00-754511-7

Amazing Scientists
978-0-00-754500-1

Amazing Writers
978-0-00-754506-3

Visit **www.collinselt.com/readers** for language activities, teacher's
notes, and to find out more about the series.